Beginner's Guide to a Head-On Collision

Beginner's Guide
to a Head-On Collision

POEMS BY

Sebastian Matthews

Red Hen Press | *Pasadena, CA*

Book design by Kim Daigle and Selena Trager

Library of Congress Cataloging-in-Publication Data

Names: Matthews, Sebastian, 1965–author.
Title: Beginner's guide to a head-on collision : poems / by Sebastian Matthews.
Description: First edition. | Pasadena, CA : Red Hen Press, [2017]
Identifiers: LCCN 2017011409 | ISBN 9781597096027 (softcover : acid-free
paper)
Subjects: LCSH: Traffic accident victims—Poetry.
Classification: LCC PS3613.A853 A6 2017 | DDC 811/.6—dc23
LC record available at https://lccn.loc.gov/2017011409
ISBN: 978-1-59709-602-7

The National Endowment for the Arts, the Los Angeles County Arts
Commission, the Dwight Stuart Youth Fund, the Max Factor Family
Foundation, the Pasadena Tournament of Roses Foundation, the Pasadena
Arts & Culture Commission and the City of Pasadena Cultural Affairs Division,
the City of Los Angeles Department of Cultural Affairs, the Audrey & Sydney
Irmas Charitable Foundation, Sony Pictures Entertainment, Amazon Literary
Partnership, and the Sherwood Foundation partially support Red Hen Press.

First Edition
Published by Red Hen Press
www.redhen.org

ACKNOWLEDGMENTS

Many thanks to the editors of the following journals in which these poems first appeared, some in slightly different form and under different titles.

American Poetry Review: "Black Hills"; *Asheville Poetry Review*: "Post-Op"; *Blackbird*: "Everything Happens to Me"; *The Café Review*: "Breaking Your Leg in Four Places"; *The Common*: "Caution in the Windy City, Thrown"; *The Georgia Review*: "Dear Virgo: 'Heart murmurs, thyroids . . . ,'" "Dear Virgo: 'I feel sorry for you, friend . . . ,'" "Dear Virgo: 'I'm getting tired of telling you . . . ,'" "Dear Virgo: 'It's not the first time . . . ,'" "Dear Virgo: 'This morning you woke . . . ,'" "Dear Virgo: 'You forget, this world is broken . . . ,'" "Dear Virgo: 'Your life is like a 4-star hotel . . . ,'" and "Dear Virgo: 'You were a tourist in the land . . .'"; *The Massachusetts Review*: "The Dead Man Returns Disguised as a Tour Guide" and "To You Who Lost Your Father"; *Miramar*: "Dear Virgo: 'Fourteen broken ribs . . .'" and "Dear Virgo: 'The scars, the doorframe . . .'"; *Mixitini Matrix*: "Beginner's Guide to a Head-On Collision" and "In Praise of the Ribcage"; *Poems & Plays*: "Jaws of Life," "Ode to the First Crash-Test Dummies," and "Watching Her at the Threshold."

to the friends, family, and neighbors who helped us through

CONTENTS

Recovering (1)

I

Recovering (2)

II

Recovering (3)

III

Recovering (4)

I have to learn alone
to turn my body without force
in the deep element . . .

—Adrienne Rich, "Diving into the Wreck"

No wonder we search for it
All our days. No wonder
We seek just a glimpse of it
And, catching that glimpse,
Are changed.

—Gregory Orr, "How Beautiful the Beloved"

You're driving up into the mountains for a weekend getaway when a sedan veers into your lane. Your car is moving approximately fifty miles per hour. So is the other automobile, which is being driven by a man in the throes of a heart attack. (The police report will say the man was dead before impact.) The sedan crosses the centerline and crashes directly into you. You shout out in surprise an instant before you're hit.

Open your eyes. Close them. Open them. The windshield is spread out on your lap in a blanket of chipped ice. Smoke oozing from car engines. Your partner is slumped in the front seat beside you, eyes shut tight. You can't tell if she is breathing. You look back at your eight-year-old boy, seated in the back behind his mother: eyes wide open, he has been brought to silence by the shock. You look back just as your wife draws a large breath.

The man and woman from the car in front of you arrive at your windows. Their teenage son takes your boy away and sits him down on a nearby grass embankment. You don't know it yet, but he has walked out of the wreck unharmed except for a minor case of whiplash and a serious seatbelt burn on his chest. Your wife, eyes clenched shut, nods when you ask if she is okay. Later, you will learn she has broken an arm, both her legs (even breaks on both tibias). One of her heels has been crushed. Your feet are both broken—one a simple ankle break, the other a more complicated set of breaks inside the foot. They remain stuck up in the well and have begun throbbing in pain. Your femur has *snapped in two places (dead center and at the hip), cracking the patella in the process. Your sternum has cracked as well, along with fourteen ribs. Later, a doctor will inform you that both your heart and lungs have been "bruised" and a small piece of spinal cord has chipped off. Lucky it didn't land somewhere it shouldn't, he will say. No obvious head injuries. No internal bleeding. You are lucky to be alive.*

I

Dear Virgo,

I feel sorry for you, friend. Maybe you should've stayed in bed.
Whose fault is it the weasel found its way into the chicken pen?
All the nice hens sit in a row; only their heads are missing.
I must confess, I drank the dregs of last night's coffee.
They were beautifully bitter. You have to resolve to go forward,
my star chart says so. But why tempt fate? There's wisdom
in reruns. I say: gather round your favorite diversions,
plump the pillows. Make sure to lock the gate.

after Marie Harris

Beginner's Guide to a Head-On Collision

Whatever you do, don't see it coming. You're too busy
doing your thing, driving to Point A, Point B. Just driving,
tunes blasting, smiling at loved ones. When the car drifts
into your lane, don't see it. Not at first. It takes a split second
for the bull's-eye to be slipped on before you understand
the simple equation of mass and force and *o shit, here
it comes*. Now the hard part's over. No, that's a lie.
It gets harder each second from here on out. Ignore
the sound of the engines sizzling like a diner grill;
no good letting your mind puzzle that one out.
More importantly, why can't you get your feet out
from under the dash, chest pressed into the wheel? What
to do about that? Breathe, man. And keep breathing. As
they take your family away, one after the other, alive, breathing,
as they pry you out of your seat like a splinter deep in.
And keep breathing on the stretcher. And in the helicopter.
Don't stop breathing, you're doing fine. We're almost there.

Grid

It lasted maybe a day, possibly two: pure bliss wrapped in metaphysic hue.
I want to write it off as what meds can do—and maybe that's all it was—
but I woke one night from dreaming, a middle-of-the night lucidity, positive
the universe was using my body as a healing grid. I could see it there pulsing.
Pain ran free in among the boxes, an AC/DC current: awareness following
close behind, dog's nose to ground. I could heal anything inside the grid
if only I could pin it there. And I did. I lay on top of the sheets, tinkering.
And in the morning, for an hour or so, I was back to my old self; I knew
I could walk again, and so could you.

Dear Virgo,

It's not the first time you've been assassinated.
You get shot all the time. Once you swilled
a poisoned martini down to the twist
before Death brimmed your brainpan
with helicopter chop and adrenaline.
Wait long enough and Resurrection comes
back in style. Your moon, though, is in
perpetual retrograde. Now's the time to act.

Watching Her at the Threshold

When I look over, she's suspended inside
a held breath I'm not sure she'll complete:

a cartoon of anticipation, she appears
desperate to emerge from such horrible

limbo. Then something releases,
her air rushes back, and here she is,

trapped like me, our boy behind us,
alive, turning her attention to the door,

the throb in her arm, to the woman
who has appeared at her window to ask

a set of life-giving questions she can begin
to form an answer to. And she speaks.

Tips on Surviving a Head-On Collision

Try not to rely too heavily on time passing swiftly. It won't cooperate. Besides,
there will come a time when you want to slow it back down. It won't do that, either.
Better leave time to its serpentine tasks. Allow for confusion inside the cockpit
bubble of pain management. Keep your finger on eject. Mistakes will be made.
Bed too short. Too much morphine. Not enough. Remember how the simple act
of breathing got you through the crash. It's there to carry you through again. Death
was waiting out in the open. You nearly drove past, but its ghost swerved at you.
Ignore the plastic tube they make you blow into. Let the words *bruised heart* blossom
into their full, clear, un-ironic truth.

Dear Virgo,

Fourteen broken ribs—7 and 7,
a turn at cracked sternum—
make quite the sonnet out of you.
Your leg throbs, your feet ache;
ribs bicker, elbowing each other
for breathing room. Pad down the hall
to pee. Wake up and—only a dream!—
piss into the bucket docilely.

Jaws of Life

This is going to hurt. An hour passes
in stutter-step fashion, lurching from calm
breath to *Get-Me-the-Fuck-Out-of-Here* gasps.
Orwellian EMTs keep coming to my window
to ask my name. They want to gauge
my consciousness. Wouldn't it be better
to articulate all the levels of pain? *What's
taking so long?* They say a broken femur is
some of the worst pain, though feet trapped
under the dash my vote for worst nightmare.
They can't get my seat unstuck, nor
can they pull the wheel from its socket.
We're going to have to get you out of here,
he says. I thought that was the point
all along. Then they have me in their arms
and are counting and, on three, release
me from my torture. Of course I scream.
And as they set my tidal body on the shore
and carry me into the sky, a new clock
gets set, a large sundial somewhere,
and a new life span starts back up.

"Poetry is a kind of faith . . .

. . . you can believe in," a friend writes in a letter. It's slipped in a card along with poems in an envelope carried all day. I re-open the letter in bed, past midnight— like peeling and sectioning an orange in a crowded bus—and reread with the focus of, well, if not prayer than all I know about caring and attention. "I just want you to know," she writes and "PLEASE KNOW" and then "Will you?" You don't have to *get* a poem. Or even care to, only willing to meet it halfway in the dark. It's the kind of openness a poem requires: risking touch with a stranger whose voice speaks in the dark, an old friend writing over telegraph wires to speak out love, praying you're still there. I fold up the letter with the poems and set them in their nest. "I can only imagine" and "if I could pray . . ." And "a wish." For now, this all I need to return to the supplication of sleep.

Dear Virgo,

Your life is like a 4-star hotel
in the process of dropping a star.
The air conditioning is out,
the bar is empty film noir; even
the elevator forgot to stop
at your floor. You can complain,
raise a fuss, or take the stairs.
Did your stay go well, Sir?

The Dead Man Returns Disguised as a Tour Guide

Come closer, step right up. The Dead Man can tell you a few things
about spectacle. Behold the beast's broken chariot, ripped apart
by jaws of steel. You heard me right, my friend, dinosaur jaws.
See how the engine sits so nicely in the lap of the automobile?!
Touch the wheel, it's still vibrating from the impact. They say
it will never stop reverberating. The Dead Man knows just a little
about shockwaves. This here is where the great bird descended
in a swirl of rain. Into which our hero was carried. I was there
to watch them vanish into the storm. You should have heard
the thunder. *Come closer.* Look carefully and you may discover
one last piece of vacation debris. The car was a swatted piñata,
a hornets' nest after the shotgun blast. The road festooned
for the parade. Here come the trucks, the sirens, the curious
souls who keep spilling from their cars, hoping against hope
to see the Dead Man one more time before he dies.

Grind

When I finally stand, three months after the accident, it is to grind coffee beans
into dust, the walker trembling for my hands. I've grown into a giant's loathing,
the little ordered world below shrunk into the distance of the tremendously
out of reach—the wheelchair a dollhouse toy. *Must I relearn everything?* My legs
are like broken cane. The kitchen light slices me in half. Left to regain my balance
I lurch for the kettle's shriek. At every turn, *Fool!* Pass into the kitchen.
Let the dog out to pee. Still a fool. Upright. Just not so gargantuan.

Dear Virgo,

I'm getting tired of telling you what to do.
Think for yourself for once. All the clichés
were true before they lost their hold.
This should be good news. You have room
to reinvent yourself. Think Houdini
creating a box to escape from, fathoms
of chains. As the air drains your chances
go up. Reemerge, or try dying.

Post-Op

The room is a circle
of muted pain.
An offshoot of time—
a new hour passing,

a button to push,
the middle finger a red baton
of silence . . .
96 95 94 95 . . .

I've become a trauma troll,
a drama doll,
the Prince of Pudding.
You are the Queen of Everything,

for whom I try not to petition;
the bearer of truth on a tray,
little white cups to deliver
what comes next:

the next little yeses
the little nos.

Shooting Hoops

First time on the court, I mince out to the free throw line like an old man.
The lights flicker to life in the murky dark. Feet on fire, right leg as stiff
as a plank, the ball a shot put in my hands. I square my shoulders, dribble it
a few times (awkward echoes around the gym), and hoist up a shot. Air ball.
Coming to a rest by a set of double doors. I hobble over and think of pushing
them open, giving up before I've even begun. No, this recovery project will be
yearlong. I've come here to heal by teaching myself how to shoot hoops again.

You wake up in a hospital bed: casted leg slung up in traction, awash in morphine, and woozy from the anesthesia. Parents bedside, fear and relief in their eyes. Two friends jumped into their car when they got the news, arrived in the middle of the night; another bullies his way into the ward after three long hours on the road. "Are you family?" "I'm his brother," he grunts, and he's not lying. Your wife is in another hospital, two hours away. Nothing makes sense.

You drift in and out of consciousness. You're taken off for another surgery but left on a stretcher in the hall for over an hour before being wheeled back to your room. The surgery has been postponed.

You don't react well to the painkillers. You start seeing things. A white cat visits you at night, floating around your bed like a tiny nurse shark in and around a reef. The nurses disappear for large stretches, won't come when you push the call button. Your feet are jammed into the baseboard, forcing you to relive the aftermath of the accident. It's driving you crazy. You imagine a conspiracy. Your mother finally raises hell with the head nurse and your too-small bed gets fixed. The doctors come around and reluctantly explain. You have become lost in the standard spiraling hell of hospitals.

In a sad version of Munchausen's syndrome, you fall in love with each new nurse who takes a shift on your floor. One brings you ginger ale and sugar cookies in the middle of the night, knowing you can't sleep.

Another brings you extra pudding. You punch at the painkiller button like they do in the television shows. A day passes, another.

Your brother comes in from the coast, stays a few days, heads back home. Your aunt arrives from New York. A modern dancer, she advises you, "The way out is through." A little too metaphysical for your state of mind. Eventually, the doctors release you from the hospital. One doc assures you that you will be reunited with your wife at a rehab center in your area. That now your son can visit you every day. You'll be there for at least a month, maybe more. You're wheeled out into the parking lot, which feels like being released from prison. Life reboots, blank screen.

II

Dear Virgo,

It's hard work getting in one's own way,
you should know. Etymologically speaking,
to be depressed is to be stuck in a rut.
A dark groove, unmotivated to rise out.
Like waking to find the basement flooded;
you dredge and bail all morning then, hands
white flags at your side, climb back up
dusty steps and set water on for coffee.

Breaking Your Leg in Four Places

The pins in your hip the size of roofing nails.
Your femur fractured twice, once at the top
and again in the middle. Your patella cracked
under the strain. Then your ankle snapped.
Though it might have gone the other way:
from gas pedal contact on up. Take your pick,
you're fucked. And your other foot mangled,
too, crushed where the toes come together
at the arch. *No more tennis,* the bone doc
quips, *unless your partner is no good.* (Though
a pro would feed you forehands in the center
of the court.) How about dancing? *Well, maybe
in a while. Let's take it one step at a time.*

Sideways

It's not memory loss exactly, nor amnesia, that empty chamber buzzing long after the bomb goes off. More like a brand of memory *displacement*, like a flood has taken the house and knocked it sideways, depositing half its contents in the backyard. Out for a night piss you place your beer down on a stump and there's your high school girlfriend, an entire volume of your friends' poetry, and the '76 Denver Nuggets' starting five, freezing in their tiny shorts, all afros and stringy white-boy hair, swaying like poorly trimmed elms.

Dear Virgo,

Even trampoliners use how-to manuals.
They turn to them with every trick.
It's a kind of mirror they look into
when unsure of their next maneuver.
Where's yours? You'll need it today
when the hours spread out, empty desert
dunes, unmapped for centuries.
Knee drop, one-half twist.

Ode to the First Crash-Test Dummies

Back in the '30s, human cadavers were thrown
down unused elevator shafts onto steel plates.
Steel ball bearings were dropped on their skulls.
In time, the cadavers were strapped into cars
wearing crude *accelerometers* and subjected to
head-on collisions, vehicle rollovers. Soon
the dummies were asked their opinions
about such things as *velocity* and *blunt force*.
There wasn't much to say at first. One caused
the other. It hurt. But some renegade CTDs
spoke of their plight. The seemingly endless
replay of death. The time they strapped a pig
into the passenger seat. They used words
like *integrity, moral code.* A few banned photos
with arms raised in defiance. *Look Ma, No Hands!*
Without these early pioneers, who knows
what pain we'd have been made to endure.
                    What velocity and force.

Caution in the Windy City, Thrown

> *It was not death, for I stood up,*
> *And all the dead lie down.*
> —Emily Dickinson

Late last night—on way back to the hotel—I walked into the mouth of a long empty alley full of dark doorways, a row of giant garage doors and a single cinematic loading dock laid out in a long shadow of lawn—Okay, I was a little drunk and stiff from a day crammed with pushing through an ever-shifting threshold of pain—walking between cars on a barreling train—and so was belligerent about my life—*I can walk through the valley of Death if I want to, thank you.* Don't worry, no hopped-up murderer popped out of the shadows. *Why chance it?* I think I needed that brand of risk—here, inside the endless present: expectancy a kind of held-breath bravado, a *ready-for-anything-bring-it-on, baby,* within the body's fuse box, its bank of sparks and shadows. I needed that runway of primordial fear, its allegorical blind alley, SOMETHING to parade my badass broken self along, stomping with brittle feet through shards of *what ifs* and *you're in the wrong place, brother, at the right time* blues. Was I asking for trouble? You tell me. Maybe a wish to be wiped clean again—beautifully rebooted but not undone. I don't know. Just that into that gap I had to go, tightrope walking the stations of danger's church, taking risk a kind of prayer. How, for those few, un-parceled moments I was . . . let's just say I disappeared into a dream rut full of bitter disasters—came out safe and clean like a washed car—a little less drunk, turned around, the hotel any which way . . . and the unmapped grid a vast maze, the elevated train rattling above and the cement under my feet singing (chorus after chorus) my unlucky and inevitable demise.

Dear Virgo,

Where were you a year ago? Stuck
in rehab? Passing a test just to get
out of bed? Remember ghosting your chair
down the hall only to whimper back
along the gangplank? Remember pushing
the beds close? Hands across the span,
feeble foreplay. Night whispers,
the extent of your lovemaking.

L'Shana Tova!

So many things to fear, so much to be sad about—
legs like brittle sticks—but not today, not now.

Old friends fill the rows alongside strangers.
This morning, you are a family. How nice

to be seated in among believers.
A woman's voice chants Torah; a string

in your hurt chest reverberates. Two wheelchairs,
an antsy boy. "Happy New Year!"

Disgust

I spend most of my time tracking down missed shots. If I shuffle too fast after an errant ball, my femur blares out a warning. The few times I execute a move to my right, bringing the basketball up high on the dribble, sharp knee pain blares. At every little jump and reach my ribcage flares. *You can't do that no more*, the body whispers. *You can't do this.* I keep my mouth shut. Start shooting foul shots. Shoot ten, make six. Shoot ten, make five. The ball keeps rimming out, hitting back iron, nicking the front of the rim, bouncing up and away. I focus on my feet, on the calf muscles, carpenter bevel breath. Shut my eyes and let the body slip into a dribble groove. Slight bend in the knees, one last backward-spinning dribble, eyes open as I come up, smooth release. Nine out of ten fall through the net. Now it's time for Around the World: shuffling around the key in an awkward dance of shoot and rebound, shoot and rebound. It takes a few minutes to get up to the top of the key; I heave the ball twice at the rim then give up in disgust.

Dear Virgo,

Fight or flight, the therapist intones. Root
impulse. Cellular tug. *But now*, she asks,
how often are you really in danger? Admit it,
hardly ever. You'd kill to wrap your hands

around that jerk's neck who cut you off.
But, of course, he's not your enemy, only
a stalking horse for something closer.
Where are you in your body? Can you feel your feet?

Everything Happens to Me

His voice warps a little, old hi-fi disc
wobbling on its tentpole axis;
the fact he no longer has teeth
broadcasting in every held syllable:
Billie's heartbreak boiled down
to shit luck and a whole carton of cigs
pressed through a grinder
to make a kind of soup out of smoke.
The song already resides in
the territory of sad sack and *o*
woe is me, but this late hour
version of Chet drenches the rag
in dishwater and squeezes it out
on the gummed floor of melody.
You can almost hear him spitting
his teeth out, beat up
from drug deal gone wrong. That
you know how he used to sing
and how he used to look
in all the old photos, pretty boy
skylark, only enhances the smirk
behind his straight face: *I'm just a fool*
who never looks before he jumps.
The voice flutters the song to a close

then drops out the window.
You peer down the alley:
there's nothing there
but the sludge line of a garbage truck.

Getting Dirty

Smiling, Della asks a simple question: "Wanna get your hands dirty?" Flats of small plants and bags of soil lie about in clusters. I've dropped off my boy at the shul, about to head to the café to write. Della and her father-in-law are getting ready to plant beds of flowers ringing the entrance steps. There's a lot of work to get done. "Sure," I say. "Why not?" The day before, on my way to pick up my son at school, passing the public golf course, a golf ball crashed into my windshield, a blur of white exploding. I shouted out but did not swerve. A beat. Then another. And then the anger came, welling up like a bottle slammed down on a table, overflowing, erupting in a primal scream. By the time I made it to the school, my heart rate was down. Only a small crack left at eye-level. When I told the story, Avery laughed nervously. I said, "Ever since the golf ball hit my windshield I've been this way . . ." Avery corrected me: "Ever since the accident, Dad . . ." Now, hands dirty, an hour in, I sweep up the soil off the steps, bring the trash around back. Della passes, more flowers to plant. "Thank you," I say. "Thank you for asking me to help."

Dear Virgo,

This morning you woke like an old man,
feet stiff and sore, knee full of ball bearings.
It's been ages since the accident, hasn't it?
Your swollen ribcage still sits on your spine
like a hive of bees ready for a new queen.
No worries. Your daily nap brings you
back, breath by labored breath. Only
those who know you can spot the limp.

King of the Rubber Guys

Not an ounce of fat on this guy. No flesh,
keyboard teeth. He's quintessential Mr. Bones.

You survived forty years shackled at the wrists.
You carry the secrets, don't you, Mr. Bones?

They're his bodyguards. Planet of the Apes,
Polar Bear. To the death they go for Mr. Bones.

His ribcage peeks through his vest. A hole
around his spinal cord. Torn pants, skin on bone.

Once you lorded over a cabinet drawer clan.
Now it's only three, minus a few rubber bones.

I let my boy play with you in the tub. *Just be
careful*, I warn. *They're fragile*. I'm weary in my bones.

What kind of boy chooses the Hunger Artist
as his superhero? You and me, Mr. Bones.

Rebirth at the Balloon Festival

The first words out of the bandleader's mouth: "We thought we left this heat behind in New Orleans." He's not complaining, more like making note of the working conditions, reminding us of his heritage. The crew was laying out a maze of ropes outside the Meadow Tent to facilitate the hot-air balloons' elephantine act of rising, still hours away, and it was too early for the crowd to slip into a summertime groove; just me and a few dozen brass band nerds waiting for the show. As usual, the crowd was mostly white in stark contrast to the dozen black men on stage, ranging in age from sixteen to sixty, though the line between us slack and eager to be rubbed out. It's been a year since our accident, an endless span of what everyone calls "recovery"—and we aren't as healed as our friends would like, though we are on our feet, wobbly but on them. My first foray back into live music since the crash, I stay off to the side as the small dance floor fills to bursting. How to describe those first few songs? A band warming up, nothing special: first show of the day, still sleepy from the drive, horns groping around in the dark for each other's sound. It feels like an old gym coming to life, its floodlights flicking on in a random grid, one fuse box switch at a time—the sacred space of hoops now alit—and by the third or fourth song ("Saints Go Marchin' In") the tent is spilling out on both sides and brimming with brio. I've shuffled up a few steps on sore feet—half in, half out. It's hard now, one year out from the head-on impact, not to take a quick inventory of that we've lost then gradually struggled to regain—the ability to walk, to take care of our boy without an army. It's a long list, the only pleasure coming in crossing off each item. But I'm not worried now as the lead drummer counts off the tempo and the band breaks into "Feel Like Funkin' It Up" and the crowd pushes deeper in and begins to groove. My own arms come off my sides, fledgling wings, and here you are, all smiles, our boy under my hands, leaning in; some space opens and our little family dances as the trumpeter stomps out counter-rhythm to the beat, and all of us let loose our worries in torrents of sweat, and I feel more reborn than anyone ever can expect, as impossibly light and majestic as the hot-air balloons that will soon float up and up and away.

You've made it out of the damn bed, the damn wheelchair, damn walker, damn house. Your eight-year-old son has been dying to get you back playing ball. He needs you back. A few steps behind in the recovery, your wife needs you back. Your students need you back. Even your aging dog yearns for a walk longer than half a block. You want to be back. But the painkillers you're tapering off fog your mind. You have a small parcel of energy for the day and no reserves. You'll come back, just not yet. When you crawl into bed, your body aches head to toe.

Rehab keeps you busy. The PTs start you off with a monotonous set of stretches. You can barely move. Can't even stand back up on your own. You're a fucking invalid. But before you know it you're hauling your underused body across the endless span of parallel bars, keeping your balance on a variety of equilibrium devices, taking your first Frankenstein steps, climbing a stage-set staircase to correct mechanics. The PTs talk you through everything, cracking jokes when you get frustrated. You let the conveyor belt of physical therapy carry you forward.

After a month, you graduate to the pool. They slide you in on this PVC pipe wheelchair, which feels like a cross between a throne and a highchair. You hide your emaciated legs under the towel. The water is warm, almost exactly body temperature, so it feels like slipping into a giant bed. At first you just float, quietly ecstatic by the surprising fact of weightlessness. But then you set your feet down. The pool bottom *tickles your soles. The water's up to your chest; you start walking. Or you start pantomiming walking. It's as if an invisible alien sits on the edge of the pool asking you to explain this whole walking thing. You put your leg up like this, you say. Toss it in front of you slowly, then shift your weight . . . But the whole shifting weight thing just doesn't feel right. You turn around and head back the other way. Your wife seems to be more adept at this strange underwater strolling. She pumps her arms out in front of her like she's jogging and, though her face is set and determined, a small smile appears at the sides of her mouth. And though you're back out in under an hour and you didn't actually do much but pretend to walk, float around and lift your legs, you can barely get in and out of the high chair. Wet noodle, you are too tired to hide your legs and more than happy to let the PT woman hold your arm as you disengage from the seat.*

III

Dear Virgo,

This is your day, brother. All signs
say so. Stars aligned, all systems go, etc.
It behooves you to undertake a project,
anything that walks you out of your head.
Build a rock wall, say. Take apart
a motorcycle. Clean the fridge, please.
It doesn't matter how, why: do something!
Let the bed ferry the dread.

To You Who Lost Your Father

I wish I could give you something from that day
you could take back to your clan. There's nothing
that hasn't been converted into personal pain.
Your father wasn't there when I encountered him,
already gone or in the throes of going. What we met
was the force of a car under the spell of momentum:
a ghost steering it into our path. Years have passed
and I keep reliving the furious, slow-motion history.
In a sense what we shared was the truth of impact—
our bodies ringing like bells in a small town
on a Holy day. I haven't been able to speak of him
until now. Haven't let myself, out of stubbornness.
How dare he hurt my family so! But I say to you
now, *Go forward under your own power. Remember him.*

Three Years Out

When we set out the rain isn't yet sleet, nor has freezing rain made the streets as brittle under boots as candy-coating in a child's fingers. I choose our standard route—past the park, up the long hill—pausing at the corner for dog to suss out sparse news before returning. But things have changed; I must pick my way from grass to rock to hedge. Looking back, I find the old dog trapped on a tilted slice of lawn unwilling to cross this new river. It feels like a dream watching the old beast make restless passes through the cold—as if spirit, separated from body, has been treed. I know this dream will end poorly so stiff-leg it back up the hill, coax the dog over the ice, and together we wind our way back.

Dear Virgo,

You forget, this world is broken
up into little societies, secret clubs
open to those who have the password
tattooed under their tongues,
in the folds of their genitals. You
gain access by exposing yourself
to gatekeeper scanners. Once you do,
do what the omens tell you to do.

In Praise of the Ribcage

In the ocean ether, an ancient, bulbous
thing lit within—sea creature, saline balloon,
thought bubble I'll float in. On land,
our unseen battle armor, secret butterfly
holding the lungs to their tidal play.
They say everything drifts back

to its source, tide-wood, mud flat,
flotsam grid—all caught in the ether,
a planet of pulsing, slowly dying light.
I say the body knows its limits, and counts
its breath one rung at a time, climbing
the ribcage back and forth into sleep.

Back

Now when I shoot hoops, I wear headphones. There's no second-guessing, no hesitation. When the ball bounces into the corner, I scurry after it. I can almost forget the years of pain and disappointment and struggle it's taken to get to this point. An old soul mix helps—"Boogie on Reggae Woman" into "Sex Machine" into "Sexy Motherfucker." That's all I need to get into a rhythm. Shoot from the corner, swish, retrieve the ball, shoot from the other corner, off the rim, grab the rebound, layup, back out to the line, swish. It's a dance, a meditation. I spin on the dribble and drive to the basket: pull up and rise for a jump shot, slight double clutch in the air. Back up, dribbling, and try again, this time spinning a little tighter, raising up a little higher. I am a sexy motherfucker. I am a sex machine. On my way out, I pass some of the players taping up in the training room. Laugh when a student makes a friendly joke about the old man limping around the court. Take the stairs two at a time, knowing I'll need to ice my ankle and pop some Advil. And head out to the car.

Dear Virgo,

You were a tourist in the land of handicap,
briefly inhabiting its space, soon to exit.
There was much to learn while there,
much to view. Still, even in the present,
you were three steps in the past,
peering in. You were inclined to look away
as much as we were not supposed
to stand and gawk at you.

Winter River, Viewed from the Bridge

We throw so much of ourselves
into the river, it's almost cliché

when the ice shards break free
and give way to the force of the current.

It feels so cathartic witnessing
this display, we can't help gushing

to one another about the river,
just this Sunday plates of ice;

how in the space of three simple days
the course has come alive, brown

and snarling; how every little thing
we give it, all our attention,

gets gobbled in its hungry mouth
and downstream spit out.

Changes

The first man crosses over the road in plenty of time—a brief head-turn to gauge distance and speed. The second man, not looking up, rushes awkwardly into the street just as I approach, causing me to tap my brakes—just enough to shoot a small jolt of adrenaline into my body. I turn my head to watch him, flushing in anger, surprised to see he's lugging a full-grown raccoon on a pole, hanging by its neck, caught in some sort of noose. The raccoon is twisting back into the man's body; both of them disappear into the quicksilver of sunlight gleaming off the corrugated metal warehouse and the river behind. The next ten minutes spent navigating on and off blaring light, made trickier by the narrow road, the approaching trucks, and the small frozen puddles laid out like mats at every driveway, turnoff, side road. Just enough heat seeps in to keep me warm but awake. Awake enough to spot, coming upon a turn, another man tightrope walking along the railroad bridge. There he is—hooded, bent forward by heavy backpack— suspended over me like an angel, backlit by sunlight, his breath puffing out of him in little train engine puffs. Then he is gone, and I am through the arches, and for a moment I lose track of what just exactly I am doing and where I might be headed.

Dear Virgo,

The scars, the doorframe scuff marks
ungainly wheelchairs leave; the limp
that reappears at day's end; the ramp,
of course, your monument to rising

out of pain. What else? "All better now,"
you say to keep the conversation on track.
There's more, you should know: memory,
old-fashioned pump, only works when primed.

Chthonic

In one version, you know where the body
is buried. In another, you bury it.

In each, the body will surely be found,
the crime unearthed. No matter what you do,

the hidden plot exposes itself—bloated
carcass rising to the surface, jawbone

sticking longways in the hound dog's maw.
Waking from these dreams (waist-deep

in sludge, coming upon locked doors)
certain you are guilty of something ghastly . . .

. . . all through the day you dread the inevitable
and mourn your ruined life. How could you have?

But this morning you sit up in the dark, calling
the dream back, imploring it to burrow deep.

Ramp

The ramp was built just days after our accident. We'd ridden our wheelchairs onto it, limped our way up and down its gentle slope—first with walkers, then canes, then on our own two legs, hands grasping the railing for support. Avery used it for his skateboard, his scooter. The dogs galumphing up and down its length. So you can't blame me if I watched the men pull down the wooden structure with barely suppressed glee, snapping pictures and cracking jokes. "The dawn of a new day," I shouted that evening to the men as they drove off. Right away, I put a chair up against the front door so no one could open it by mistake and fall. The next morning I opened the door to see again an entrance free of such dark and haunting memories. It wasn't an hour later, the dogs itching for a walk, that I walked up to the door, attaching leashes to collars, crouching, eager to get out into the sunny day, pushing the chair out of the way, opening the door . . . and falling . . . body turning in the air, arms out to brace, one slipping down into a foundation hole. The dogs jumped down after me, sniffing at my face in confusion. *What have I just done?* I stood up slowly, checking my body for possible breaks, cuts, gashes. My left arm was already aching at the wrist. My whole left side was sore. But no real blood to speak of, no broken bones. I'd missed by a few inches hitting my head on a cement block. I dusted myself off and picked up the leashes and limped my way out onto the road. By the time I got back to the house, I was stiff and sore. The dogs jumped right up, but I had to slide my body up into the entranceway then maneuver it awkwardly over the threshold.

Dear Virgo,

Heart murmurs, thyroids gone mad.
The cancer's in remission, the swelling
has subsided. Everywhere you go
people are in the throes of living.
So follow your dreams, sweet dear,
even the one that swerves into hell.
You remember that nightmare?
Fighter, shrinking ring, and final bell.

On the Way to Spruce Pine

On our wall, a photo snapped the day
we collected you. Looking over my shoulder

to make sure you were safe. Flash-forward
eight years to this day: heading deep into

the mountains to celebrate a family becoming.
Remember the end-of-day light? The car floating

into our lane? Some part of us remains, lost
on that mountain road—halfway between

home and weekend vacation—shadow family
stranded roadside: homeless, bereft,

picking through the car's ghost body
for fragments of a stopped life. This, too,

a photo, though no one snapped it.
Nonexistent caption scrawled on windshield.

Black Hills

Not the abruptly slowing cars ahead, nor the way traffic snarled to a standstill, now inching forward as the right lane merged with the left; not the blinking lights ahead, nor the ambulance sprawled sideways across the lanes; not the men and women huddled in the breakdown lane; not even the one automobile, turned over on its hood, door ajar. None of it stirred my son and his friend from their video game cocoon, never once looking up to see, happy in each other's parallel play. ("It's when you buy the moon," one says to the other. "This game gets fun.") And on the way back from the match, late afternoon light cutting sideways across the lanes, visor down to block the blare, I passed the exit for 221, the road we crashed on at just this hour, heading up to Spruce Pine for a weekend getaway. I kept us straight on 40, letting the quiet music carry me forward; and as we headed up the mountains, the stench of burning brakes from the trucks coming down, with the sun now bright and triumphant behind the Black Hills calling out the oncoming night in trumpeting reds and yellows, even I didn't look up from my cocoon of driving and notice all the potential wreckage, even I didn't flare up in my own body or lose hope for the future.

When you are still in your chair, your son coaxes you outside to witness him jump on the trampoline. You've been watching the Summer Olympics, following the volleyball matches. He starts knocking a beach ball around inside the circular net. He throws it up and catches it in midair, spiking it. You wheel closer. He throws you the beach ball. You catch it and throw it back. A game starts up. You try to throw it so he can't catch it. He dives and lunges. A natural athlete, he quickly covers every angle, reading the trajectory as soon as it's out of your hands.

When you graduate to a walker, he makes you reach a little. You've learned where to throw the ball so he can't get it. ("Dad, trampolines don't have corners.") There's a little trick of using the tape at the top of the net to divert the ball's path. He becomes the master of the shoestring catch. Now you're on your own two feet and he starts placing the ball so you have to take a few steps to grab it. You get two bounces. A week of hard work, of getting your feet to pick up off the dirt and pivot, of applying what you're learning on the basketball court, and you graduate to one bounce.

When you're able to move around a little, the play area you patrol expands. You replace the beach ball with a soccer ball. You come up with a point system. Rules about serves. Do's and don'ts. Your boy has stopped playing nice. You can reach just about anything he sends your way. He always wins. It doesn't matter. You dub the game "Butterfingers" and begin to envision it becoming an Olympic sport, *you and your son the heroic pioneers. But, truly, you give thanks to the trampoline for providing such an elastic and flexible arena. And you don't tell him, but you see your boy as one of your trainers.*

You stay out until it's so dark the ball starts to disappear into the tree shadows. Until you're both called in for dinner.

GRATITUDES

Thanks to . . .

Ali and Avery, for sharing this amazing ride with me, and allowing me to include you (once again) in these dispatches. I love you both so much.

Marie Harris for her work on the Bruised Heart collaboration and for understanding when I needed to break it. That book lives behind and inside this one.

Curtis Bauer and Vievee Francis for being such good friends and for serving as the initial audience (and as editors) to many of these pieces.

Alex Long and Ryan Walsh for sharing morning lines with me and Curtis.

Keith Flynn, A. Van Jordan, and Dana Levin, who inspire and bolster me by who they are and the work they do.

Charter Weeks for his powerful and disturbing photomontages to match mine. And for being there through thick and thin.

Kevin McIlvoy and Emilie White for being not only loyal supporters of my work but also good friends and such amazing writers themselves.

Matthew Olzmann, Ross White, and all the "Grinders" I shared the ever-valuable Grind with.

Maggie Anderson for insisting that "Black Hills" was a poem.

Ross Gay and Patrick Rosal for their interest in "Recovering" and their own amazing, badass poetry.

Landon Godfrey and Gary Hawkins, for being so cool and so dedicated.

Laurie Corral and Landon's Vandercooked series at Asheville Book Works for including me in such a creative, nurturing scene.

Paul Moxon for his elegant and creative broadside of "Dear Virgo: 'It's not the first time...'"

Jen Acker, Gaylord Brewer, Christopher Buckley, Stephen Corey, Luke Hankins, Ata Moharreri, Emilia Phillips, Elizabeth Scanlon, and Pamela Uschuk and William Pitt Root for helping me see that these poems were more than therapeutic and pushing them out in the world.

Donna Read, dear friend, for training me and helping me remember that the way out is indeed through.

Gary Clark and the staff at the Vermont Studio Center for providing such necessary sanctuary for so many people, including myself.

Mark E. Cull, Selena Trager, Hannah Moye, and the crew at Red Hen Press for putting this thing together so expertly.

And, of course, Kate Gale, who saw the book I was writing, backed it enthusiastically, and pushed me to dig deeper.

Biographical Note

Sebastian Matthews is the author of a memoir and three books of poetry. His work has appeared in *American Poetry Review, Atlantic Monthly, Georgia Review, The Sun,* and *Virginia Quarterly Review,* among others. He is currently working on a collection of personal essays and a book of prose poems. Matthews chairs the Vermont Studio Center trustee board and serves on the advisory board of *Callaloo: A Journal of African Diaspora Arts & Letters.*

His graphic "collage" novel, *The Life & Times of American Crow,* is available at www.americancrowgraphicnovel.com.

Printed in the USA
CPSIA information can be obtained
at www.ICGtesting.com
JSHW081123110823
46380JS00001B/3